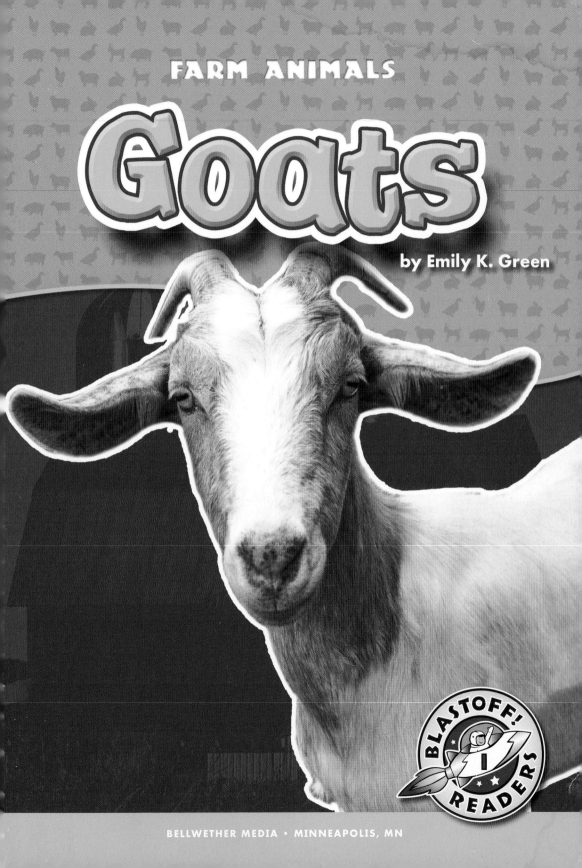

FARM ANIMALS

Goats

by Emily K. Green

BELLWETHER MEDIA · MINNEAPOLIS, MN

BLASTOFF! READERS

Note to Librarians, Teachers, and Parents:

Blastoff! Readers are carefully developed by literacy experts and combine standards-based content with developmentally appropriate text.

Level 1 provides the most support through repetition of high-frequency words, light text, predictable sentence patterns, and strong visual support.

Level 2 offers early readers a bit more challenge through varied simple sentences, increased text load, and less repetition of high-frequency words.

Level 3 advances early-fluent readers toward fluency through increased text and concept load, less reliance on visuals, longer sentences, and more literary language.

Whichever book is right for your reader, Blastoff! Readers are the perfect books to build confidence and encourage a love of reading that will last a lifetime!

This edition first published in 2007 by Bellwether Media.

No part of this publication may be reproduced in whole or in part without written permission of the publisher. For information regarding permission, write to Bellwether Media Inc., Attention: Permissions Department, Post Office Box 1C, Minnetonka, MN 55345-9998.

Library of Congress Cataloging-in-Publication Data
Green, Emily K., 1966–
 Goats / by Emily K. Green.
  p. cm. — (Blastoff! readers. Farm animals)
Summary: "A basic introduction to goats and how they live on the farm. Simple text and full color photographs. Developed by literacy experts for students in kindergarten through third grade"—Provided by publisher.
 Includes bibliographical references and index.
 ISBN-13: 978-1-60014-066-2 (hardcover : alk. paper)
 ISBN-10: 1-60014-066-1 (hardcover : alk. paper)
 1. Goats—Juvenile literature. I. Title.

SF383.35.G74 2007
 636.3'9—dc22   2006035305

Text copyright © 2007 by Bellwether Media.
SCHOLASTIC, CHILDREN'S PRESS, and associated logos are trademarks and/or registered trademarks of Scholastic Inc.
Printed in the United States of America.

Contents

A goat is a
farm animal.

A female goat is a **doe**. A young goat is a **kid**.

kid

A male goat is
a **billy goat**
or a **buck**.

A goat's **pupil** is the shape of a rectangle.

pupil

Both male and
female goats
may have beards.

17

Female goats
give milk. Farmers
must milk their
goats every day.

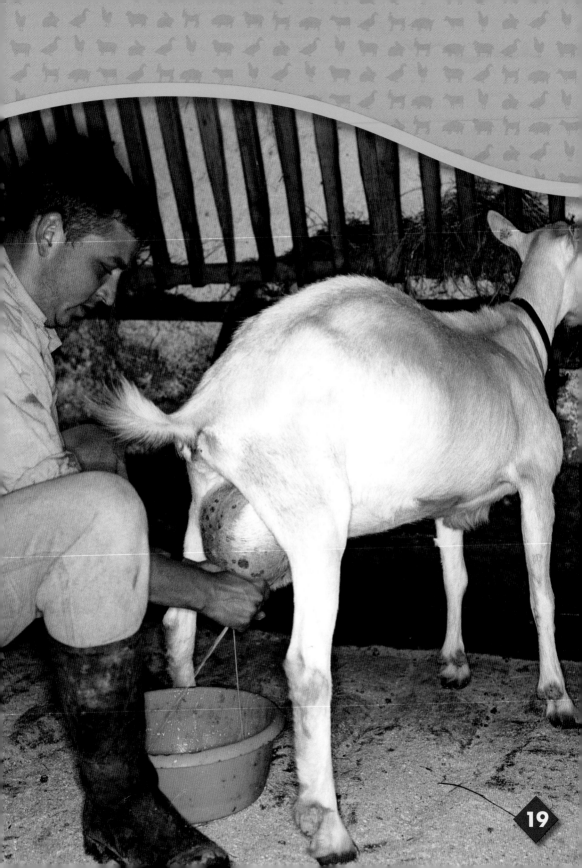

Goats are
great climbers.
Some goats
even climb trees.

Glossary

billy goat—a male goat

buck—a male goat

doe—a female goat

kid—a young goat

pupil—the center part of the eye

To Learn More

AT THE LIBRARY

Barber, Tom. *A Tale of Two Goats*. New York: Barron's Educational Series, 2005.

Gugler, Laurel Dee. *There's a Billy Goat in the Garden*. Cambridge, Mass.: Barefoot Books, 2003.

Rix, Jamie. *Giddy Goat*. Grand Rapids, Mich.: Gingham Dog Press, 2003.

ON THE WEB

Learning more about farm animals is as easy as 1, 2, 3.

1. Go to www.factsurfer.com

2. Enter "farm animals" into search box.

3. Click the "Surf" button and you will see a list of related web sites.

With factsurfer.com, finding more information is just a click away.

Index

The photographs in this book are reproduced through the courtesy of: Mlenny, front cover; Patricia Doyle/Getty Images, p. 5; Anette Linnea Rasmussen, p. 7; Frank Krahmer/Getty Image, p. 9; Hans Neleman/Getty Images, p. 11; Val Corbett/Getty Images, p. 13; Phil Schofield/Getty Images, p. 15; Sven Wever/Alamy, p. 17; Erik Dreyer/Getty Images, p. 19; plainpicture/Endless image/Alamy, p. 21.